鳥 山 明

Happy New Year! I made my debut as a manga artist on my 23rd New Year, and now, as I write this, I'm facing my 30th. I guess somehow I've "made it" as a manga artist. This is a tough business—if you've got work to do then you are so busy that there's no time to sleep. If you don't have any work, then you don't have anything to do *but* sleep. I don't like to be too busy, but I also don't like to be in a bind, so I try to keep working hard.
—*Akira Toriyama, 1986*

Artist/writer Akira Toriyama burst onto the manga scene in 1980 with the wildly popular **Dr. Slump**, a science fiction comedy about the adventures of a mad scientist and his android "daughter." In 1984 he created his hit series **Dragon Ball**, which ran until 1995 in Shueisha's best-selling magazine **Weekly Shonen Jump**, and was translated into foreign languages around the world. Since **Dragon Ball**, he has worked on a variety of short series, including **Cowa!**, **Kajika**, **SandLand**, and **Neko Majin**, as well as a children's book, **Toccio the Angel**. He is also known for his design work on video games, particularly the **Dragon Warrior** RPG series. He lives with his family in Japan.

DRAGON BALL Vol. 2
Gollancz Manga Edition

STORY AND ART BY AKIRA TORIYAMA

English Adaptation/Gerard Jones
Translation/Mari Morimoto
Touch-Up Art & Lettering/Wayne Truman
Graphics and Design/Sean Lee
Cover Design/Izumi Evers & Dan Ziegler
Editor/Jason Thompson & Trish Ledoux
UK Cover Adaptation/Sue Michenwicz

DRAGON BALL © 1984 by BIRD STUDIO
All rights reserved.
First published in Japan in 1984 by SHUEISHA Inc., Tokyo.
English publication rights in United Kingdom arranged by SHUEISHA Inc.
through VIZ Media, LLC, U.S.A and Tuttle-Mori Agency, Inc., Japan and Ed Victor Ltd., U.K.
This edition published in Great Britain in 2005 by Gollancz Manga,
an imprint of the Orion Publishing Group, Orion House, 5 Upper St Martin's Lane,
London WC2H 9EA, and a licensee of VIZ Media LLC.

1 3 5 7 9 10 8 6 4 2

The right of Akira Toriyama to be identified as the author of this
work has been asserted by him in accordance with the
Copyright, Designs and Patents Act 1988.

A CIP catalogue record for this book is available
from the British Library

ISBN 0 575 07736 0

Printed and bound at Mackays of Chatham, PLC

www.orionbooks.co.uk

SHONEN JUMP GRAPHIC NOVEL

DRAG★N BALL

Vol. 2

DB: 2 of 42

STORY AND ART BY
AKIRA TORIYAMA

THE MAIN CHARACTERS

Son Goku
Monkey-tailed young Goku learned kung-fu and inherited the magic *nyoi-bō* staff from his grandfather Gohan. Bulma is the first girl he ever saw.

Yamcha
A martial artist and bandit, Yamcha intends to steal the Dragon Balls from our heroes. His one weakness is that he's scared of girls.

Oolong
Immature, shapeshifting Oolong can change into anything, but only for five minutes at a time. He used to be a villain, but now he has (against his will) joined our heroes.

Pu'ar
Yamcha's shapeshifting friend.

Bulma
A genius inventor, Bulma created the Dragon Radar which detects the location of the Dragon Balls.

Bulma

Pu'ar

Yamcha

Son Goku

Oolong

Gyû-Maô
The fearsome lord of Fry-Pan Mountain, Gyû-Maô, aka the "Ox King", has been known to deal harshly with trespassers.

Gyû-Maô

Kame-Sen'nin (The "Turtle Hermit")
A mystical dirty old man who gave Goku the *kinto'un*, or flying cloud, and gave Bulma the third Dragon Ball, in return for helping his turtle friend.

Kame-Sen'nin

Chi-Chi

Chi-Chi
A strange girl who Yamcha and Pu'ar ran into. She has a tendency to overreact.

Deep in the mountains lived an innocent boy named Son Goku, until he was found by Bulma, a girl from the city who was searching for the seven magical Dragon Balls. According to legend, when all the Dragon Balls are brought together, Shen Long – the eternal dragon – will appear and grant any one wish. When Bulma saw how strong Goku was, she convinced him to join her on the adventure. Now, they have gathered five of the seven Balls, and along the way, they have met many strange people and things…

DRAGON BALL 2

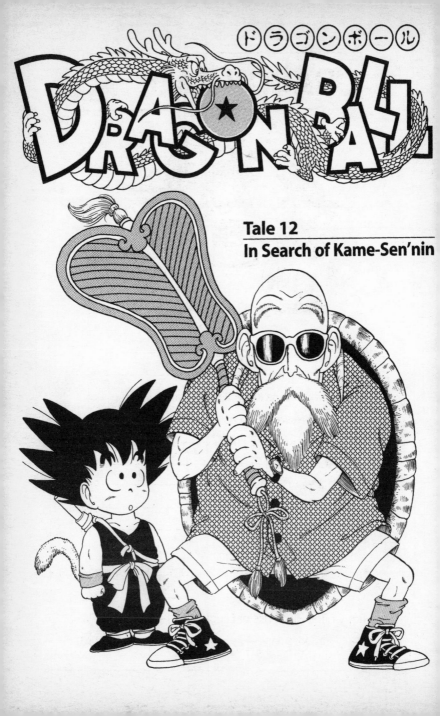

ドラゴン・ボール

DRAGON BALL

Tale 12
In Search of Kame-Sen'nin

GYŪ-MAŌ, THE "OX KING," HAS SEEN GOKU'S KIN-TO'UN... AND REVEALED THAT THE STINKY OLD WEIRDO WHO GAVE IT TO HIM IS REALLY HIS "MUTEN-RŌSHI," HIS MASTER OF LONG AGO...KAME-SEN'NIN, A.K.A. THE TURTLE MASTER!

THAT "MUTEN..." WHATEVER... YOU MEAN THE TURTLE GUY, RIGHT?

WE KINDA KNOW, DON'T WE?

I-I-I-I THINK IF WE GO TO THAT B-BEACH...

YEAH!! I'LL BE ABLE TO GET BACK IN MY CASTLE!!

WOO-HOO!!

HEY!! ARE YOU GOAN TELL ME WHERE MY INVINCIBLE OLD MASTER LIVES OR AM I GOAN KILL YA?!

HUH...?!

8

YUP!!

Y-YOUR... ?! WAS HIS NAME *SON GOHAN*?!

WOW, YOU'RE GOOD! MY GRAMPA GAVE ME THIS!

TH-THAT STAFF YOU GOT...IS THAT THE "NYOI-BŌ"...?

SHEESH... HE'S JUST *FULL* OF SURPRISES...

--I WAS RIGHT! THAT KID *IS* IN TIGHT WITH GYŪ-MAŌ!

YOU KNEW MY GRAMPA ?!

HOO-HOO-*HOO*!! DON'T THAT BEAT ALL!! SON GOHAN'S *GRANDSON*!!

N-NOW I'M STARTING TO SEE WHY HE'S SO STRONG...

FOR *REAL*?!!

..."*KNEW* HIM"?! SONNY BOY, M'LORD MASTER'S #2 STUDENT WAS *ME*... AND HIS #1 WAS YOUR *GRANDPA*!!

I STILL CAN'T BELIEVE THAT OLD PERV WITH THE TURTLE WAS ACTUALLY *SOME-BODY*...

MAN, THAT BRINGS BACK MEMORIES--!!

9

ACCORDIN' TO SOURCES THAT SHALL GO UNNAMED, I MIGHT BE ABLE TO PUT OUT THAT BIG MOUNTAIN-FIRE WITH A DEVICE CALLED A "BASHŌ-SEN" THAT MY OL' LORD OWNS.

WHAT IS IT?

PAP

ENOUGH O' THIS!!

MEMORIES CAN WAIT! I GOT A *FAVOR* TO ASK YOU!

IT LOOKS A LOT LIKE THIS.

DON'T YOU HAVE ONE IN YOUR CASTLE?

"DRAGON BALL"? WHAT'S THAT?

SURE! WILL YOU GIVE US THE DRAGON BALL FOR IT?

C'DJOU MAKE A QUICK FLY-BY ON THE KIN-TO'UN TO BORRY THE THING AN' BRING IT BACK HERE?

MY FIRST SIGHT OF A DRAGON BALL... TINY LI'L THING, ISN'T IT...

I FIGURED THEY'D BE AT LEAST AS BIG AS DODGE-BALLS...

BANZAI!!

YAY!!

I'M GONNA *LIVE*, I'M GONNA *LIVE*...

SURE, SURE, NO SWEAT!! FOR WHAT *I* WANT, THAT'S *NOTHIN'*!!

OHH...YEAH, YEAH, NOW THAT YOU MENTION IT, I THINK I'VE SEEN ONE OF THOSE...

WHOA!! WAIT A SEC!

THEN I'LL GET *GOING*!!

10

CHI-CHI?

IF YOU RUN INTO HER ON THE ROAD, HOW 'BOUT TAKIN' HER ALONG?

NOT THAT I THOUGHT IT'D DO ANY GOOD, BUT YESTERDAY I ALREADY SENT MY DAUGHTER, CHI-CHI, OUT LOOKIN' FOR THE OLD MASTER.

TAKE A LOOK AT *THIS*, SONNY!!

SNORT

WHAT'S A "WIFE"?

SHE'S A HOT-HEAD, BUT SHE'S A CUTIE! HOT*CHA*! I COULD GIVE HER TO YA AS YOUR *WIFE*!!

EEP?!

WHOA-HOA!! SHE SURE DOESN'T TAKE AFTER *YOU*!!

SO I SHOULD BRING THAT KID ALONG WITH ME... RIGHT.

A-A-AND SHE'S THE DAUGHTER OF THE *GYŪ-MAŌ*...!!

L-LORD YAMCHA... TH-THAT GIRL... SH-SHE'S THE ONE YOU JUST KONKED ON THE HEAD...!!

12

HOW DO YOU KNOW MY NAME...?!

HUH?!

W-WAIT, PL-PLEASE, MISS CHI-CHI!

SHAA

--"LOVE"? F-F-F-FOR *WHO*? FOR *ME*?!

YEAH... RIGHT...

WH-WHAT MATTERS IS... I WANT TO APOLOGIZE FOR...YOU KNOW...

I-I-I-IT DOESN'T MATTER...

PL-PLEASE FORGIVE ME! I WAS JUST... SO CRAZY WITH *LOVE* THAT...

LOOK AT THIS FACE! IS THIS THE FACE OF A LIAR?

YOU'D BETTER NOT BE *LYING*!

........!!

EWWWW! YOU'VE GOT A TOOTH MISSING...I DON'T KNOW IF YOU'RE A LIAR, BUT YOU'RE SURE WEIRD-LOOKING...

EASY, LORD YAMCHA... EEEEASY... JUST THIS ONCE...!

GRINN

WHEN YOU'RE IN LOVE YOU'RE S'POSED TO GO ON A "DATE"...

I READ ABOUT IT IN A MAGAZINE ONCE...

AND YOU HOLD HANDS...

SHOOT!! HE'S COMING!!

AK !!

WOW...NO ONE'S EVER SAID HE LOVED ME BEFORE...

BWOON

HIDE !!

HUH ?

I CAN'T *STAND* IT !!

EEE EEE !!

HUH ?

...I KNOW! HE MUST BE AS SHY AS I AM!

WHA HAP- PENED... ?

HE LEFT... ?

14

...AND HE KNOWS MY NAME ALREADY TOO...

SOME-BODY ELSE I'VE NEVER MET...

IS YOUR NAME "CHI-CHI"?!

AHOY!

HUH?!

?

?

--I GET IT!! *YOU* MUST BE IN LOVE WITH ME TOO!!

...AND HELP YOU GO BORROW SOMETHIN' FROM SOMEBODY.

YUP. HE SAID I SHOULD PICK YOU UP...

NO! *REALLY*?!!

HUH?! YOU KNOW MY DAD?!

HEY. YOU'RE TH' OX KING'S KID, RIGHT?

THEN I'M *ON!* MY HEART'S AS CLEAN AS AN INDOOR TOILET!!

WELL... ONLY IF YOUR HEART'S CLEAN AN' PURE...

Y-YOU CAN RIDE THAT...THAT BALL OF COTTON CANDY?

C'MON, GET ON MY KIN-TO'UN AN' I'LL TAKE YOU.

HURRY UP AN'...

OOMPHA...

HUH?

NN... NN... NNNNNNNNN...

...OKAY, I'M ON.

I CAN'T HELP HAVING WHAT I HAVE, CAN I?

WELL WHAT'RE YOU DOIN' WITH A TAIL, ANYWAY?!

DON'T SQUEEZE MY TAIL, WILL YA...? IT MAKES ME LOSE MY STRENGTH...

OWW...

WH-WHAT HAPPENED?

VICTORY IS SURELY OURS!!

HIS WEAK SPOT IS HIS *TAIL*!!

HEH HEH HEH... WHAT A LUCKY BIT OF LISTENING...!

16

HANG ON TIGHT!

WHOA--!!!

THEY'LL RETURN TO TAKE THE SIXTH DRAGON BALL...

JUST WHAT WE'RE DOING.

WHAT DO WE DO NOW, LORD YAMCHA?

...AND WHEN THEY BEGIN HUNTING FOR THE SEVENTH ONE, WE'LL BEGIN TAILING THEM AGAIN.

FAST, HUH?!!

...I'LL TAKE THEM WITH MY "FIST OF THE WOLF FANG."

THE MOMENT THEY'VE GATHERED ALL SEVEN...

HYUUUNNN

GAH!! I *HATE* DENTISTS...!!

IF WE HAVE SOME TIME, MAYBE WE SHOULD GO TO A DENTIST.

IT'S ALL THAT STUPID GOKU-KID'S FAULT!!

!!

PAT PAT

...

...

YOU DON'T HAVE A BOY'S WEE-WEE, DO YOU? YOU MUST BE A *GIRL!*

GET YOUR HAND *OFF ME!!!!*

BOMF

WAAH!!

EEEE- EEEE !!!

GUH!!!

DOOF

GOMP

OWW...

...

YOU DID *PLENTY*!!!

WHAT DID I DO TO DESERVE THAT?

BLUSH

BUT, THOUGHT THE MAIDEN, HAVING BEING TOUCHED "THERE," WHAT ELSE COULD IT MEAN BUT THAT SHE WOULD BECOME THIS YOUTH'S WIFE...?

I SURE HOPE LITTLE GOKU WAS ABLE TO FIND MY DAUGHTER

I WISH IT WAS *ME* FINDING HER...

AS LONG AS HE HASN'T TRIED THE "PAT-PAT"...

NEXT: YOUR BIGGEST FAN!

IF ANYTHING CAN KILL THE BLAZE ON FRY-PAN MOUNTAIN, IT'S THE MYSTERIOUS OBJECT ON THIS ISLAND...BUT...

OF COURSE IT IS! I GOT IT STRAIGHT FROM KAMI-SAMA HIMSELF!*

THIS KIN-TO'UN YOU GAVE ME IS *AWESOME*!!

KAME HOUSE

Tale 13
Fanning the Flame

...HASN'T SHE SHRUNK A LITTLE?!

H-HEY, LAD... THE GIRL WITH YOU...

HUH ?!

HEY--! DIDJA HEAR THAT!? KIN-TO'UN IS LIKE FROM ANOTHER WORLD...!

Y'KNOW WHAT I MEAN ?

BOING!

I MEAN, LAST TIME I TOOK A LOOK AT HER, SHE WAS A LOT MORE... MORE...

*ONE WAY OF SAYING "GOD," TORIYAMA'S "KAMI-SAMA" ISN'T MEANT TO STAND IN FOR A FIRE-AND-BRIMSTONE JEHOVAH, BUT AS AN OTHERWORLDLY POWER OF OBSCURE ORIGIN. —ED.

YER NAME'S CHI-CHI, RIGHT?

WHAT? THIS IS *HIS* DAUGHTER?! CAN IT BE?!

NOD NOD

THIS IS GYŪ-MAŌ'S KID!

HUH...? NO, NO!

...!!

I'M NOT...?

YOU'RE *NOT* TELLING ME THAT THAT OLD CREEP IS REALLY THE MUTEN-RŌSHI!

WOULD'VE BEEN A BETTER NAME FOR THE *OTHER* ONE...

"CHI-CHI," *HMM*...?*

MY DAD'S *REAL* MASTER OUGHTTA BE ABLE TO DODGE THIS...

?

ONE IS CHI-CHI... AND ONE *HAS* CHI-CHI'S... THAT MAKES TWO CHI-CHI'S... NO, THREE...

fsh

I'M GONNA PUT HIM TO THE TEST...

HUH?

HSSH

HYAH!!!...

*AS YOU MAY BE ABLE TO GUESS FROM KAME-SENNIN'S MURMURINGS, "CHI-CHI" IS A JAPANESE BABY-WORD FOR "BREASTS." COMPLICATING IT FURTHER IS THAT IT'S ALSO A WORD FOR "FATHER."

...THE "BASHŌ-SEN"! THAT'S THE WORD!

D'YOU HAVE... *UM...*

HUH? OH! RIGHT! I FORGOT!

...WHAT BROUGHT YOU HERE, ANYWAY?

ANYWAY... GOKU...

THE MAGIC *FAN* THAT CAN RAISE A TYPHOON WITH A SINGLE WAVE, A THUNDERSTORM WITH TWO, AND A MONSOON WITH THREE?! *THAT* BASHŌ-SEN?!

WHAT?! THE BASHŌ-SEN?!

WE'LL BRING IT RIGHT BACK, AND WE WON'T LET IT GET BURNED!

WE NEED IT TO PUT OUT FRY-PAN MOUNTAIN'S FIRE!!

JUST TO *BORROW*!

YES, I HAVE IT... BUT WHAT DO *YOU* WANT IT FOR?!

I'VE HEARD RUMORS... AND IT'S POSSIBLE, YES...THE BASHŌ-SEN MIGHT BE ABLE TO...

HMM... I SEE... FRY-PAN MOUNTAIN'S FIRE, EH...?

WHAT IS THERE TO THINK ABOUT?

PLEASE!! PLEASE!! PLEASE!!

PLEASE!!

...

...I HAVE ONE CONDITION!!

HOW-EVER...

YAY!! THANK YOU SO MUCH!!!

...IT IS AGREED!! I SHALL LEND IT TO YOU!!

I'LL LEND YOU THE BASHŌ-SEN, SO...

WHAT IS IT?

"CONDITION"...?

ME?

UM... COME OVER HERE...

C'MON... JUST A SEC... OVER HERE...

YOU MEAN BULMA, RIGHT?

...THE ONE YOU WERE WITH LAST TIME... THE BOINGY ONE...

Y'KNOW THAT GIRL...

28

YOU JUST WAIT WHILE I GET THAT FAN!

ALL RIGHT, THEN!! NOW THAT *THAT'S* SETTLED...

SURE.

THIS IS OUR LITTLE SECRET, EH? NO NEED FOR CHI-CHI TO KNOW... OR ESPECIALLY GYÛ-MAO...

TSK TSK TSK...

OH, D-DON'T FRET YOUR HEAD... IT'S ALL BEEN SETTLED...

SO WHAT'S THE CONDITION...?

SOME PEOPLE HAVE SOME WEIRD IDEAS OF FUN...

A...P-P-POT-HOLDER...?

IF I'M NOT MISTAKEN YOU WERE USING IT AS A POTHOLDER, SIR.

THAT'S FUNNY... HEY, TURTLE! DO YOU KNOW WHERE I PUT THE BASHÔ-SEN?

I SPILLED SOME WONTON SOUP ON IT... AND IT WAS SO STAINED I THREW IT AWAY!

YOU DON'T MEAN THAT... WAS THE *MAGIC FAN*?! FOOEY!

29

GUESS WE'LL GIVE UP ON THE DRAGON BALL TOO...

WAAAH!! NOW WE'LL NEVER GO HOME!!

YOU THREW IT... AWAY?!

WHAT--?!

NOT ONE OF HIS BETTER MOMENTS...

SINCE THE FAULT IS MINE...I WILL PERSONALLY TRAVEL TO FRY-PAN MOUNTAIN AND PUT OUT THE INFERNO!!

NEVER FEAR!!

LISTEN, YOU LET BULMA KNOW ABOUT THE... Y'KNOW...NICE 'N' QUIET, WILL YOU?

YOU KNOW IT!!

OLD TIMER... CAN YOU REALLY DO THAT...?!

WHAT?!

OF COURSE I CAN! THERE'S NOTHING THE MUTEN-RŌSHI CAN'T DO!!

30

32

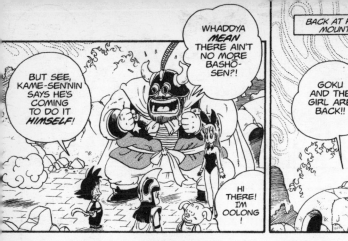

BUT SEE, KAME-SEN'NIN SAYS HE'S COMING TO DO IT *HIMSELF!*

WHADDYA *MEAN* THERE AIN'T NO MORE BASHO-SEN?!

HI THERE! I'M OOLONG!

BACK AT FRY-PAN MOUNTAIN...

GOKU AND THE GIRL ARE BACK!!

HOT *DANG*!! MY INVINCIBLE OLD MASTER!! LONG TIME NO SEE!!

...

LOOK, THERE HE IS, THERE HE IS!

GWOOO

DOMP

KWR KWRR

HOW'S HE GOING TO PUT OUT THE FIRE? BY *HURLING* ON IT?! STAY TUNED FOR...

...

RETCH RETCH BLARG

OOOH, I HATE FLYING...

HWAA

ALL OUR HOPES ARE ON *HIM*...?

NEXT: *KAMEHAMEHA--!!*

DRAGON BALL

ドラゴンボール

Tale 14   Kame Kame Kame Kame Kame Chameleon

THE AUGUST MARTIAL ARTS MASTER NAMED KAME-SEN'NIN HAS AGREED TO QUENCH THE INFERNO ON FRY-PAN MOUNTAIN BY HIS OWN POWER! (HECK, SINCE HE SPILLED WONTON SOUP ON THE MAGIC FAN, WHAT *ELSE* COULD HE DO?) HE DOES, HOWEVER, HAVE CERTAIN... *CONDITIONS.*

GROOAR....

GYŪ-MAŌ!

HEY!

AND YOU CAN PUT *THAT* OUT?

HOOO-EE! THAT'S AN *INFERNO,* ALL RIGHT!

Y-Y-YES, SIR!!

ALAS, MASTER!! Y-Y-YOU SPEAK TRULY!!

THOSE *TREASURES* OF YOURS COST A FEW *LIVES*, I HEAR...

GETTIN' A *BAD REP* LATELY, EH...?

WELL, LET'S NOT GO *OVER-BOARD*...

I'VE SEEN THE LIGHT!! IF YOU DOUSE THAT FLAME, I WILL *DESTROY* MY TR-TREASURES!!

OH, THE SHAME I BEAR!! I-I-I HAVE BEEN BLINDED BY GREED!!

TSK TSK TSK... I'M JUST DISAPPOINTED YOU CAN'T PUT OUT THAT TINY LI'L BLAZE YOURSELF...

NOW *THAT*... I THOUGHT I'D *NEVER* SEE...!

HUH?

THE AGREEMENT, REMEMBER...?

HEY-HEY!

BUDDY!

OH... YEAH...

POKE POKE

36

C-C-C-CAN YOU STEP OVER HERE A SECOND...? TH-TH-THE REST OF YOU CAN WAIT...

?

WHAT IS IT...?

HUH? ME?

HEY, BULMA! THE TURTLE GUY WANTS TO ASK YOU FOR SOMETHIN'!

ahem

ahem

WHAT?!

?

?

OKAY. THE OLD GUY WANTS TO PAT-PAT YOUR CHEST.

G-G-GO ON, LAD, Y-Y-YOU ASK HER...!

UNLESS FIRE GO BYE-BYE... LITTLE GIRLIE NOT GET HER DRAGON BALL, HMM...?

I CAN'T *BELIEVE* YOU!! WASN'T LAST TIME BAD *ENOUGH*?!

...OR *I* WON'T PUT OUT THE FIRE! NYAH! NYAH!

J-J-J-J-JUST ONE LITTLE H-HARMLESS F-FEEL...

GOKU, YOU IDIOT! JUST DO A TV COMMERCIAL ABOUT THE DRAGON BALLS, WHY DON'T YOU?!

ARRRHHH...!

37

38

39

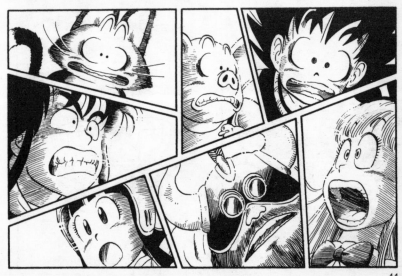

AMAMAMA... MAZING...!

THAT WAS A BIG'N...

PHEWW...

45

NEXT: OUT OF *FRY-PAN...AND* THE *FIRE...*

Tale 15
At Sixes and Sevens

FOR MONTHS NOW, POOR GYŪ-MAŌ AND CHI-CHI HAVE BEEN SUFFERING BECAUSE THEY COULDN'T GET TO THEIR OWN HOME! AND NOW...WELL...THEY CAN **GET** TO IT...
ZOOM IN!
K-CHIK K-CHIK...
'KAY... WE'RE HERE, SO...A LEETLE TO THE SOUTH-WEST...
AN' IN **THIS** WE HAVE TO FIND A BALL...
OH, QUIT WHINING! I STILL HAVE THE DRAGON RADAR!

50

51

...I SEE WHERE HE GOT HIS TRAINING...

HO HO HO... NOW THAT I WATCH HIM...

...GOHAN MENTIONING A KID HE'D PICKED UP... WITH A *TAIL*...

UH-OH. I WRECKED THE CAR...

Y'KNOW, I DO REMEMBER, ONCE...

--*DEAD!!* OH, MY, OH MY... WHAT A LOSS...

OKAY, I GUESS. HE'S DEAD.

SO HOW'S OLD GOHAN DOIN', LADDIE?

AS SOON AS WE GET THE LAST TWO DRAGON BALLS, I'M *THERE*!!

REALLY ?!

IN THAT CASE, M'BOY... WOULD YOU LIKE TO MOVE IN WITH ME? YOU MIGHT OUTDO ME, ONE O' THESE DAYS!

TH-THE MASTER *NEVER* TAKES DISCIPLES ANYMORE...! TO BE CHOSEN BY *HIM*... BRRRR!

IT JUST GETS WORSE, DOESN'T IT...?

PSHAW! WE'LL JUST HAVE TO *TAIL* THEM-- SO TO SPEAK-- AT A SAFE DISTANCE.

B-BUT THE CAR WITH THE HOMING DEVICE! I-IT'S BEEN...

ARE YOU KIDDING?! NOT AS LONG AS WE KNOW THE *SECRET*-- OF SQUEEZING HIS TAIL!!

WELL, I GUESS THAT TAKES CARE OF THE GREAT DRAGON BALL SCHEME...

IT'S THE CHII-SHIN-CHŪ !!!

1...2... 3...4... 5...6...

I'VE *GOT* IT!!!

AWRIGHT! THEY MUSTA FOUND IT!!

WHOO-HAH!

WHOOPEE!

54

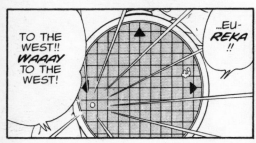

WHO?! ME?!

OOLONG. I NEED TO TALK TO YOU...

UH-HUH

CAN YOU HOLD ON FOR A SEC, PLEASE?

I HAD TO PROMISE THAT OLD PERVERT I'D LET HIM TOUCH-TEST MY CASSABAS IF HE'D PUT OUT THE FIRE AND WE GOT THE D-BALL.

OKAY, IT'S LIKE THIS...

YOU... WHAT?!

JUST C'MERE, WILLYA?

WH-WHAT IS IT?

?

I'M NOT HAVIN' ANYTHING TO DO WITH THIS!! NO *WAY* I'M LETTING THAT OLD FREAK EVEN GET *CLOSE* TO ME!!

A-A-ARE YOU KIDDING?!!

WAK !!

SO HOW 'BOUT YOU ADOPTING MY FORM AND LETTING HIM PROD *YOU* INSTEAD?

SOMETHIN' TELLS ME YOU'RE *NOT* GONNA DIE A PRETTY DEATH...

• • •

THEN YOU'D RATHER I TRIGGER THE OL' *FWEEE* REFLEX?!

OH, REALLY?

GOING?! ON?! N-NOTHING!! NOTHING AT ALL!!

UH... WHAT'S GOIN' OAN?

BA-BUMP BA-BUMP

ZHEE ZHEE

BLUSH BLUSH

GULP!

WHAT COULD BE T-TAKING THEM SO LONG...?

GOD YOU'RE VAIN...

GYAAH!! WHAT ARE TRYING TO DO?! HAVE YOU EVER ACTUALLY LOOKED AT ME?!

BOMB!

HOW'S THIS?

OH, COME OFF IT...

GASP !! WHAT A SHOCK! I WAS ABOUT TO ASK WHAT A MOVIE GODDESS WAS DOING IN THIS WASTE-LAND...!!

YOU CAN'T COMPLAIN ABOUT THIS!!

OKAY... NOW?!!

HEL-LO-O-O-O!

HEE HEE

OH, I'M *SO* SORRY ♡!

YOU BAD, BAD GIRL! YOU KEPT ME WAAAAITING!!

I ACTUALLY THINK THIS "OLD MASTER" IS EVEN SLEAZIER THAN *ME*...!

VROOOOOOOM!!

OH, COME NOW! YOU MEAN YOU REALLY JUST WANT TO *POKE* AT THEM?!

EH?

L-LET ME AT 'EM...!

heh heh heh...

O-OKAY, THEN...

BBUMP BBUMP

P-PUFF... P-PUFF...?

WOULDN'T YOU RATHER... GET TO *PUFF-PUFF*?!

PUFF-PUFF!!

...AND GO... "PUFF-PUFF"!

YOU PUT YOUR FACE RIGHT IN BETWEEN...

UH-HUH UH-HUH

TA-DAA!!

YOU *IDIOT*!! WHAT'RE YOU *DOING* TO ME?!

PUFF-PUFF! PUFF-PUFF! HERE I COME...

GWAAAH!!!

WHERE THE PUFFING NEVER STOPS!

WHUHH--!!

PUFF PUFF PUFF!

UHH...!!

JUST PUFF AWAY!

HEY, GOKU.

AREN'T THEY DONE YET...?

I GOT A *REPUTATION* TO PROTECT, Y'KNOW!!

YOU'RE GONNA *PAY* FOR THIS, GEEK!!

P'TWONG

NNNNG...

Today... I Consider Myself...

...the Luckiest Man Alive.

...I'LL BE SURE TO COME AN' GET! COUNT ON IT!

WELL, WHATEVER HE WANTS TO GIVE ME...

OH, COME ON! DON'T PLAY INNOCENT!

HUH? HE'S GONNA GIVE ME SOMETHING?

...I'LL BET MY FATHER WOULD GIVE YOU MY HAND.

WHEN YOU'RE OLD ENOUGH...

IF I REMEMBER RIGHT, WE HAVE A CAPSULE FOR A *NEWER* MODEL THAN THEIRS...THE SILVER STAR MARK 4!! LET'S SWITCH!!

ARRH!! WE CAN'T KEEP UP!!

I CAN'T *WAIT* TO SEE THAT DRAGON... !!

SO...WE'RE FINALLY DOWN TO THE LAST DRAGON BALL!

AT LAST, THE MOMENT DRAWS NEAR WHEN ALL THEIR WISHES WILL BE GRANTED! ON THE OTHER HAND, YOU KNOW WHAT THEY SAY ABOUT BEING CAREFUL WHAT YOU WISH FOR...

NEXT: RABBIT EARS

BULMA, GOKU, AND OOLONG HEAD EVER WESTWARD...IN QUEST OF THE LAST REMAINING DRAGON BALL!!

HYOUOONNN

Tale 16
One Goal, One Enemy

AARGH! AND NOW WE'RE RUNNING OUT OF FUEL...!

HEY, OOLONG! IS THERE A CITY OR ANYTHING AROUND HERE SOMEWHERE?

WHAT A WEIRD PLACE THIS IS...

I DUNNO... I'VE NEVER GONE THIS FAR...

SHOOOOONNNN

SO YOU'RE ABOUT TO COMPLETE YOUR DRAGON BALL COLLECTION...

HEH HEH HEH...

JUST DON'T LOSE SIGHT OF THEM, NO MATTER WHAT!

AYE AYE, SIR!!

N-N-NO!! PLEASE!! I-I-IT IS ON THE *HOUSE!!*

HUH?

YOU'LL HAVE TO WAIT TO GET PAID. THE ONE WITH THE WALLET'LL BE BACK SOON.

TH-THANK YOU... Y-YOUR TANK IS FULL...

PL-PLEASE... F-FORGIVE ME...!

HMM... NOT MUCH ON SELECTION, ARE YOU...?

OH, *NO!! NO!!* TH-THERE'S NO CHARGE, OF COURSE!!

HOW MUCH ARE THEY?

S'OKAY. I'LL JUST TAKE THESE FIVE.

COULD YOU NUMBER 'EM AND PUT 'EM IN A CASE?

CAPSULES

66

...NOT PART... OF THE R-RABBIT MOB...?

Y... YOU'RE...

WHAT'S THAT?

RABBIT MOB?

SO THIS IS THE BEST YOU'VE GOT, HUH...?

WELL, I GUESS ANYTHING BEATS THAT BUNNY GIRL OUTFIT...

...

DON'T TELL ME IT WAS BECAUSE OF THE BUNNY EARS...?

EVERY-BODY'S STOPPED STARING...

ACTUALLY... *YOU* ARE!

I SUPPOSE THIS IS YOUR IDEA OF A *JOKE*!!

TOO BAD I DON'T HAVE TIME FOR A TERRIFIED HEART-FREEZE! COME ON, BOYS!!

AT LEAST NOW I UNDERSTAND WHY PEOPLE WERE RUNNING AT THE SIGHT OF ME EARLIER.

YOU MUST BE NEW AROUND HERE.

OH, COME ON! THERE'S NO HEART THAT DOESN'T FREEZE IN TERROR AT THE NAME OF "THE RABBIT MOB"!

HEY, GOKU. THESE ARE BAD GUYS. BEAT 'EM UP FOR US.

OKAY.

I GUESS YOU NEVER WANT TO SEE OLD AGE!

CHHH-K

OHH, A FEISTY ONE, EH?

WHAT--?!

ARE YOU *NUTS*?! THEY GOT *GUNS*!!

YOU'RE GONNA "BEAT US UP"?!

N...NO ONE... MAKES FUN... OF THE RABBIT MOB...

UNNH... OWWW... !!

...I WISH *MORE* IDIOTS WOULD ATTACK GOKU!

HEH HEH HEH... YOU KNOW...

WHAT'S THAT DOPE MUMBLING ABOUT NOW?

WE'VE COME UP AGAINST... A REAL STRONG ONE...

M-MASTER... SORRY TO TROUBLE YOU...BUT WE NEED YOU!

A CLOUD OF TERROR DESCENDS UPON THE TOWN... JUST WHO *IS* THIS MASTER OF THE RABBIT MOB?!

HUH ?!

HOW CAN WE EVER THANK YOU...FOR BRINGING *DOOM* ON US *ALL*?!

WAAAA—

R-RUN! RUN FOR YOUR LIVES--!!

AIIEEE--

NEXT: BOSS BUNNY!

THAT'S GRATITUDE FOR YOU! BEAT UP THE TOWN BULLIES AND PEOPLE THANK YOU...BY RUNNING LIKE HECK! MAKES YOU CURIOUS TO MEET THE HEAD OF THE RABBIT MOB...DOESN'T IT?

WAAH-- RUN--! HIDE--!!

WHAT'S GOING ON?!

WH...WH... WHAT...?

Tale 17
Carrot Top

HELP ME THINK OF A REASON THAT ISN'T TERRIFYING...

THEY'RE ALL... GONE...?

YOU ALL RIGHT, BIG BUDDY?

UHHH...

THEY COULD HAVE THANKED US, AT LEAST!

WELL, I NEVER!

"BOSS"...?

DON'T WORRY!! I CALLED THE BOSS!!

TH... THAT... KID...!!

CARROTS..?

HEH HEH HEH... YOUR ASSES ARE GRASSES...

HEY!! WHO IS THIS "BOSS," ANYWAY?!

NAH! THEY'RE CARROTS! AN' THEY'RE ABOUT TO GET NIBBLED! HA!

78

79

WHRRRRRRR

HO-YO--!!

SHWA

TMP

WAAH!!

IS THIS GUY FOR REAL...?!

HUH?!

PRESS THE FLESH, CUTIE.

DON'T *TOUCH* HIM!!

I REMEMBER!! HE'S TH-THE *CARROT MASTER!!*

HAH!! AS IF A BABE LIKE *ME* WOULD SHAKE HANDS WITH A *RODENT*!!

PWAP

TOO LATE, CHICKIE. WE TOUCHED.

HEH HEH HEH...

NOW DO YA GET IT?

BOMF

NYAH NYAH, TOLD YOU SO! TOLD YOU SO!

HA HA HA!

AAGH!! BULMA TURNED INTO A CARROT!!

I'M TOO LATE...!! I COULDN'T WARN HER... ABOUT HIS TOUCH!!

81

OR MAYBE ALL YER LIFE YOU'VE WANTED TO BE A CARROT!

SO YOU WANNA MIX IT, EH, BUD?

CHANGE HER *BACK*, YOU!!!

TM

USE THAT STICK O' YOURS!! THEN YOU WON'T HAVE TO TOUCH HIM!!

WAIT !!

DON'T !!

WH... WHUH...

FWASH

GAAH !!

GOOD THINKIN' !!

HEY, THANKS !!

HERE'S THE CARROT!

OWW!!
OWW!!

OWW!!
OWW!!

POO

pap pap

OKAY !!

HUH ?

OKAY!! OKAY!! WHATEVER YOU SAY!!

OKAY!! CHANGE IT BACK TO BULMA AND I WON'T KILL YOU!!

M-MASTER, DON'T TOUCH ME! I DON'T WANNA BE A CARROT...!

OWWW...

YAMCHA AND HIS FRIEND CAME AND HELPED US!

WHY DO I FEEL SO... ORANGE...?

OOO, THAT WAS CLOSE...! TO THINK I WAS NEARLY RIGHT NEXT TO A...BRR... GIRL!

HUH? HE WAS JUST HERE A MINUTE AGO...

HIM?!! THAT HUNK?! WHERE IS HE?!

OKAY, STAFF!! STRETCH A LONG WAY!!

WAAH!!

JAB

AIEE--! HAVE MERCY...!!

NOW, WHAT TO DO WITH YOU THREE...

NEXT: STOLEN BALLS!

Tale 18 • Who's Got My Balls?!

WA-HA! IT'S IN THE BAG!

SHUU~~...N

WHAT'S WRONG WITH **YOU**?! YOU SMELL DANGER AND GO **AFTER** IT!

WHAT'S WRONG WITH YOU, ANYWAY? EVERY TIME YOU SMELL DANGER, YOU GO RUNNING AWAY!

AFTER YOU GET ALL THE DRAGON BALLS, WHAT ARE YOU GONNA **WISH** FOR?

HEY, BULMA... I'VE BEEN MEANING TO ASK YOU...

A BOYFRIEND!!! THE WORLD'S GREATEST BOYFRIEND!!

HO HO HO!! HAVEN'T I TOLD YOU YET ?!

90

NOT JUST A "CHICK"... *ME*! YOU SHOULD BE PROUD TO CONTRIBUTE TO SUCH A WORTHY CAUSE!

TO HELP A CHICK FIND A *BOYFRIEND*?!

WAITA-MINNIT!! Y'MEAN I'VE BEEN RISKING MY *NECK*--

...AND ONE CAR HAS JUST PASSED THROUGH.

LORD PILAF! I AM IN AREA H-15...

YES, M'LORD!!

THAT'S GOT TO BE THE ONE!! COMMENCE THE OPERATION!!

SO BA, SO GOOD!

--SOBA! CAN YOU SEE THE CAR?

...THE DRAGON BALLS !!

THEY'VE GOT THEM...

OH, SHUT UP!! WHAT HAVE *YOU* DONE FOR ME, ANYWAY?!

AFTER EVERYTHING WE'VE BEEN THROUGH-- COULDN'T YOU AT LEAST USE THEM FOR SOMETHING *WORTHWHILE*?!

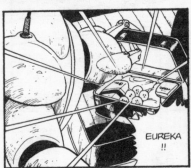

96

DOMP

WELL?! *SAY* SOME-THING!

POKE

I SHOULDN'T BE SURPRISED THAT OTHERS KNOW ABOUT THE BALLS...

THEY WERE CHRONICLED IN ANCIENT DOCUMENTS, AFTER ALL...

I GUESS...

WHAT A WEAKLING...

HE JUST... DIED!

YOU *ARE* NUTS !!

OKAY, HOW 'BOUT THIS? *I'LL* BE YOUR BOYFRIEND!

ARE YOU *NUTS* ?!

C'MON! LET'S JUST GIVE UP! THIS TIME WE'RE REALLY SCREWED!

SO WHAT'S THE NEWS ?!

HEY !!

YOO-HOO...

THEN WHAT ARE YOU DOING BACK *HERE*?!

WEREN'T THERE.

AND THE BALLS...?!

I TOOK HIM OUT!

I STILL GOT MINE.

OH !!

FOOLS!! YOU'VE MISSED ONE!! *NYAH, NYAH!!*

WA-HA-HA !!

WAAH!! THEY'VE PROBABLY GOT THE LAST BALL ALREADY!!

WITH THE STOLEN ONES, THEY'VE GOT ALL *SEVEN!!*

...AND IT SHALL STILL BE *I* WHO CLAIMS THE DRAGON'S *WISH!!*

NOW WE'LL USE THE DRAGON RADAR TO FIND THE THIEVES' LAIR...

AK !!

TH-THE CAPSULES... TH-THEY WERE IN THE BAG... WITH THE BALLS...!

YOU UNDERESTIMATE ME, BUCKO! I BOUGHT CAPSULES AT THE LAST TOWN!

GREAT... EXCEPT HOW DO WE GET THERE WITHOUT A *CAR?*

MY DRAGON BALLS... STOLEN... !!

I-IT LOOKS LIKE THEY WERE STOLEN, ALL RIGHT...

WAA! WAA!

OHHHH!! YAMMM-CHA!!

OH! YAMCHA !

...MY MY *MY*!! WHAT A TOTAL COINCIDENCE!! WHAT ARE *YOU* DOING *HERE?*!

IT CAN'T BE HELPED...WE'LL HAVE TO LEND THEM A HAND AGAIN...

99

100

IT'S A DEAD END...

HUH?

WHAT?! WHAT IS IT?! WHAT?!

LET'S GO SEE...

WE'RE TRAPPED!!!

YAAGH~!!

KLATTA-KLATTA

DMM

THREE HEROES...TWO VILLAINS...UNITED IN DESPERATION! SEE WHAT HAPPENS WHEN THE SEVEN DRAGON BALLS ARE UNITED, TOO!!

WELL... THAT WAS EASY...

...

I NEVER BELIEVED THERE **WERE** PEOPLE THAT STUPID...

NEXT: *A BIT OF RICE ON THE SIDE*

Tale 19
At Last...
the Dragon!

HAVING STOLEN THE DRAGON BALLS, THE WOULD-BE WORLD CONQUERORS OF THE **REICH PILAF** HAVE NOW CAPTURED BULMA AND COMPANY... (WITHOUT A GREAT DEAL OF DIFFICULTY, WE SHOULD ADD)...

HEH HEH HEH...! SOON, NO LEADER ON EARTH SHALL ACT WITHOUT AN **ORDER OF PILAF**!!

WHAT?! THAT MEANS...ONE OF THEM HAS IT **ON** HIM... OR **HER**!

LORD PILAF! THE DRAGON BALL ISN'T IN THE CAR!

THERE'S NO WAY **OUT**!!

I **TOLD** YOU WE SHOULDN'T COME IN HERE!!

I CAN'T EVEN PUNCH THROUGH IT...

PERHAPS BETWEEN THOSE MEN'S LEGS, SIR...

STRANGE, THOUGH... THERE'S NO SIGN OF A *BALL*...

YOU KNOW WE DO NOT APPRECIATE VULGAR HUMOR HERE...

MY APOLOGIES.

...

AFTER ALL, *SOME* MANGA CREATORS STRIVE TO MAKE THEIR WORK DIGNIFIED AND REFINED!!

S-SIR, I...

...ESPECIALLY DR SLUMP* REFERENCES !!

AK !!

YES, MY LORD!!

BUDDA-BING!

...THEN YOU ARE VERY SADLY MISTAKEN !!

IF YOU THINK WE'LL PANDER TO OUR AUDIENCE'S SHAMEFUL LOVE OF PEE-PEE, KAKA HUMOR SIMPLY TO BOOST THE SALES OF THIS *DRAGON BALL* COMIC...

*AKIRA TORIYAMA'S FIRST RECORD-BREAKINGLY POPULAR SERIES WHICH RAN IN JAPAN FROM 1980 TO 1984.

HE **NOSE** WE'RE SCARED...

...BUT LET **SNOT RUN**!!

...

YOU'RE JUST JEALOUS BECAUSE **YOU** CAN'T THINK OF A PUN THAT CLEVER!

IF YOU'VE GOT THE ENERGY TO MAKE **BOOGER JOKES**, MAYBE YOU'VE GOT THE ENERGY TO THINK OF A WAY **OUTTA** HERE!!

LORD YAMCHA... UNLESS I'M MISTAKEN, WHAT YOU JUST SAID...

...WAS A PUN!

OH?!

I AM PILAF THE GREAT!!

HEY! YOU!!

...

HONESTLY...! I TRY TO LIGHTEN THE MOOD A LITTLE, AND WHAT DO I GET...?!

HEY, IF WE BREAK THAT WINDOW, WE CAN GET OUT!

YOU IDIOT! THAT'S A TELEVISION!

ALL... EXCEPT FOR *ONE*, MY DEAR!!

SO YOU'RE THE ONE WHO STOLE *MY* DRAGON BALLS!!

GIVE IT TO ME NOW... AND YOU WILL REMAIN ON THE *SIDE OF PILAF!!*

YOU HAVE THE BALL WITH FOUR STARS IN IT!!

POP

HUH ?!

GRRR... !!

I'LL TAKE A SIDE OF UDON! AS IN... *U DON* GET NOTHIN'! NYAH!

I'M GOING TO DO SOMETHING *NASTY...!!*

VERY WELL, THEN...IF YOU REFUSE TO CO-OPERATE...

108

NOOOO...!!

GLOMP

EEK !!

WHOA... COOL...

WHAT'S HE MEAN BY "NASTY"?

UH-OH... THIS COULD BE TROUBLE...!

HEH HEH HEH... IF YOU HAVE ANY HOPE OF AVOIDING SHAME...TELL ME WHERE THAT *BALL* IS!!

LET ME *GO*, YOU MUGGERS !!

WHADDA YOU THINK YOU'RE GONNA *DO?*!!

SO YOU LIKE BEING SUBJECTED TO HUMILIATING ACTS, EH...?

FEH!! I GOT JUST *ONE THING* T' TELL YOU, RUNT--

H-HANG IN THERE, G-G-GIRL!! W-WE'RE WITH YOU!!

ALL RIGHT, THEN...

HOO-WAA!

...AHEM.

...HUH?

GROSS!

EWWW!

...E AND THE "K" WORD!

I-I-I-I BLEW YOU A *KISS*...!!

WHAT *WAS* THAT...?

A-ARE YOU R-READY TO TALK *NOW*?!

W-WELL?!!

YEAH? AND...?

THE WAY THINGS ARE GOING, I FIGURED YOU WERE GONNA STRIP ME NUDE AND DO A "SLURP-SLURP" OR A "PUFF-PUFF" OR A "PAT-PAT" OR EVEN A "GROPE-GROPE"!

phew...

HUH?!

THAT'S TELLING HIM!

...E'S A PERV!!

H-HOW CAN YOU EVEN STAND TO *THINK* OF SUCH HIDEOUS THINGS!

AAUGH!!! WHAT A DISEASED MIND!!

LORD PILAF, WHAT ABOUT KNOCKING THEM OUT WITH SLEEPING GAS AND THEN SEARCHING THEM?

I FEAR WE'RE UP AGAINST SOMETHING FAR MORE TERRIBLE THAN WE'VE EVER IMAGINED...

OWW!!

BOMPF

I'M GLAD YOU'RE LEARNING FROM ME. NOW GET TO IT!

PRECISELY WHAT I WAS ABOUT TO ORDER!!

HAK HAK WAAH--!!

WH-WHERE'D THIS SMOKE C...CCCC...

SPI//~~SH

OH!!

NOW WHAT...?!

WHEE!!N

BUHHH...

DRAG... GON... BUH...

NOW LET'S GO FIND THAT... THAT DRA...

HA HA HA... SLEEPING LIKE BABIES!

OH DEAR, OH DEAR...

STAY WITH HIM... I'LL FIND THAT DRAGON BALL...!

DUMF!!

OH!! LORD PILAF !!

HE FORGOT TO PUT HIS GAS MASK ON!

HMM... WHERE TO START...

AH-
HA
!!!!!

WHA~
?!

STILL
FEELING...
A LITTLE
BOILED...

GLUH...

YES,
SIR
!!

BUT YOU DID
WELL, MY
KERNELS!
I MEAN...
COLONELS!
ALL SEVEN
ARE
OURS!

AND NOW...
HEE HEE HEE...
THERE SHALL
BE NO
POWER ON
EARTH *OVER
PILAF!!!*

HYAH!!!

IT'S TOO LATE...!! HE PROBABLY GOT HIS WISH GRANTED WHILE WE WERE STILL KNOCKED OUT...!!

MY KICKS DON'T DO ANY GOOD, EITHER.

IT'S NO USE!! THE WALL'S TOO SOLID--I CAN'T BREAK THROUGH !!

I-I-IS THIS ANY TIME TO WORRY ABOUT TH-THAT?! JUST DO IT!!

BUT HOW DO *YOU* KNOW ABOUT THAT?

THE KAMEHA-MEHA!! THAT TRICK THE OLD MASTER SHOWED YOU!!

WAIT!! GOKU!!

OH, YEAH !

I'LL DO IT.

OKAY, OKAY.

GET READY...

GULP...

I-I'M ABOUT TO SUMMON THE DRAGON GOD...

BOOF

--HA !!

HA... ME...

KA... ME...

D-KOOM

HEY!! THEY'RE OUT THERE!!

AND IT LOOKS LIKE THE *DRAGON* HASN'T APPEARED YET!!

WHAT?!!

OOPS.

I DON'T HAVE A LOT OF PRACTICE. I THOUGHT THE HOLE WOULD BE BIGGER.

STEAL BACK THE DRAGON BALLS FROM THEM WHILE THERE'S STILL TIME!!

PU'AR!! TRANSFORM INTO A BAT AND FLY THROUGH THIS HOLE!!

YOU'RE *SOOO* BRILLIANT!!

CAN DO!!

WH-WHO?! ME?!

HUH?!

WHAT ARE YOU JUST STANDING THERE STARING FOR?!! OOLONG, GO WITH HIM!!

BOM!

I'LL GO. I'LL GO, I'LL GO, I'LL *GO*!!

WHY DON'T YOU MAKE YOURSELF USEFUL FOR ONCE?! OR ELSE... *SWEE-SWEE-SWEEE...!!*

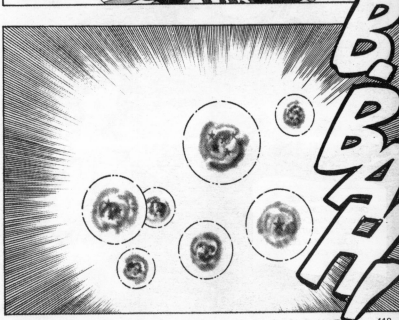

118

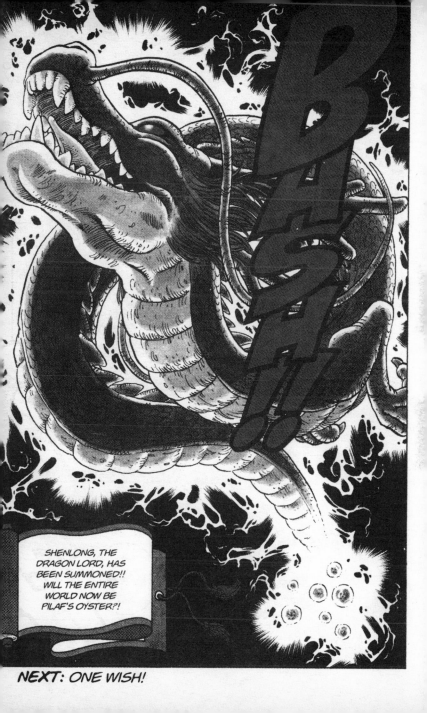

SHENLONG, THE DRAGON LORD, HAS BEEN SUMMONED!! WILL THE ENTIRE WORLD NOW BE PILAF'S OYSTER?!

NEXT: ONE WISH!

BSHOOOM

Tale 20
Just One Wish!!

KRAKKL

KRAKKL

THE *REICH PILAF'S* RECIPE FOR ABSOLUTE POWER: TAKE ONE DRAGON BALL OF THEIR OWN, MIX WITH SIX STOLEN FROM OUR HEROES, SUMMON THE DRAGON SHENLONG...AND THIS WORLD IS *COOKED!*

THE PANTIES OFF A HOT BABE !!!

126

WOOOOOO...

NYAH NYAH!! THAT'LL TEACH YOU!!

THAT LITTLE PIG *DID* IT!!

'COURSE I PLANNED ON THIS ALL ALONG!

HEH HEH HEH...

HEH... HEH HEH

WHEN A WISH IS GRANTED, THEY SCATTER AGAIN ALL ACROSS THE WORLD.

THE DRAGON BALLS ALL FLEW OFF EVERYPLACE!! LIKE... *BLAM!!*

...BUT THAT'S HOW IT WORKS...

SORRY...

YOU MEAN THE BALL MY GRAMPA LEFT ME TOOK OFF *TOO*?!

129

YES SIR!!

OFF WITH THEIR *HEADS*!! OFF!! OFF!!

I WANT THAT PIG AND THAT CAT-- *NOW*!!!

YOU CALL THAT AN *ESCAPE* ATTEMPT...?

WE COULDN'T HELP IT. THEY HAD LASER BLASTERS...

DROOP

WE WON'T BE SMASHING THROUGH ANY WALLS *THIS* TIME...

THIS ROOM IS CON-STRUCTED OF PURE STEEL...

TANG TANG

HAA!!!!

POING

SO WHAT?! THE *TOP'S* WIDE OPEN!

UH-UH... THAT'S SHATTER-PROOF GLASS UP THERE.

TOLD YOU SO.

OW!! OW!! OWWW--!!

KANG

WHAT?

WE CAN'T GATHER 'EM AGAIN FOR A WHILE ANYWAY...

...WE'LL BE DEAD! AND THEN WE'LL *NEVER* BE ABLE TO GET THOSE DRAGON BALLS AGAIN...!

BLAST IT...IF WE DON'T FIND A WAY OUT OF HERE...

ONCE A WISH IS GRANTED, IT SUPPOSEDLY TAKES AT LEAST A YEAR FOR THOSE SEVEN BALLS TO BECOME DRAGON BALLS AGAIN...

UNTIL THAT YEAR PASSES, THEY'RE JUST ROUND ROCKS... AND THERE'S NO WAY TO TRACK THEM...

YES! ANOTHER WHOLE YEAR OF BEING TERRIFIED AROUND GIRLS...!

THIS IS GONNA BE ONE DULL COMIC BOOK...

A YUH-YUH-YUH... YEAR...?!

NOW THERE'S A PROBLEM...

YOU HAVE ALL SEALED YOUR *DOOM*!!!

HOW *DARE* YOU DAMPEN MY DREAMS OF CONQUEST JUST WHEN THEY WERE ABOUT TO *BOIL*?!

...SO I WILL LET YOU DIE VERY *SLOWLY*!!

BUT DON'T WORRY...HEH HEH HEH HEH... PILAF IS A MILD AND TENDER MASTER...

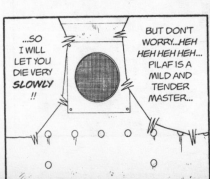

132

NEXT: My APE is UP!

IT'S ALWAYS DARKEST
BEFORE THE DAWN...
BUT IN THIS CASE,
THE DAWN BRINGS
A DEATH-DEALING
SUMMER SUN!!

Tale 21
Full Moon

POUND 'EM, BLAST 'EM,
RAH RAH RAH!!

TANG TANG

BSHH

ESCAPE
IS
IMPOSSIBLE...
!!

HE...
HE'S
RIGHT...
!

THOSE WALLS
ARE FOOT-
THICK STEEL
SHEETS! THE
CEILING IS
STATE-OF-THE-
ART GLASS!!
NOT EVEN A
CANNON CAN
PIERCE IT!!

BWA HA HA!!
STRUGGLE
ALL YOU
WANT, YOU
FOOLS!!

FOR THOSE
WHO CANNOT
SWALLOW THE
ORDERS OF
PILAF...THE
END IS
DEATH!!

YES SIR!

IT'S GETTING LATE...I SHOULD GET SOME SLEEP...

I WANT TO BE *FRESH* FOR TOMORROW... !!

HEE HEE HEE HEE

SO THIS IS HOW IT ENDS, HUH...?

TOO HUNGRY... NO STRENGTH...

CAN'T... GO ON...

huff

huff

HUH...?

SO TELL ME WHO *DOES*!!

NO!! I *REFUSE*!! I DO *NOT* LIKE DYING!!

HOW CAN YOU CARE ABOUT THE *MOON* AT A TIME LIKE THIS?!

I'M LOOKING AT THE MOON.

PU'AR... WHAT THE HECK ARE YOU DOING?

FULL MOON, HUH...?

DON'T *SAY* THAT!!

I WANT TO SEE SOMETHING PRETTY BEFORE I DIE.

IT'S A FULL MOON, THAT'S HOW.

WHAT'RE WE, TELLIN' CAMPFIRE STORIES?

OH, YEAH, RIGHT...A WEREWOLF, I'LL BET.

A HORRIBLE MONSTER COMES WHEN THE MOON'S FULL, YOU KNOW!!

IT'S *TRUE*!! MY GRAMPA DIED FROM BEIN' *STEPPED* ON BY THAT MONSTER!!

I DIDN'T SEE IT. I WAS ASLEEP.

WHAT KIND OF MONSTER **WAS** IT?

AN' MY **HOUSE**!! AN' THE **TREES**!! **EVERYTHING**!!

YOU'RE TELLING ME IT **SMASHED** THE LEGENDARY MARTIAL-ARTS MASTER SON GOHAN...?!

"NEVER LOOK AT THE FULL MOON, BOY"...

GRAMPA ALWAYS USED TO SAY...

WHAT ARE YOU **MADE** OF, ANYWAY?!

YOU **SLEPT** THROUGH YOUR **HOUSE** BEING DESTROYED?!

ONLY I DON'T KNOW WHAT ME **LOOKIN'** AT IT COULD DO...

WHAT'S WRONG?

HUH?

...

I WONDER IF THAT MONSTER COMES OUT AROUND HERE, TOO...

T-T-T-TELL ME SOMETHING...

TH-THE NIGHT YOUR GRAMPA DIED...DID YOU LOOK AT THE M-MOON...?

I-IT C-CAN'T B-BE...

M-M-ME...?! WH-WH-WHAT DO **YOU** THINK...?!

WH-WH-WHAT DO YOU THINK...?

HE TOLD ME NOT TO, BUT WHEN I WENT TO PEE... WELL...

YEAH !!

C-C-COULD BE JUST COINCIDENCE... C-COULDN'T IT...?

'C-C-COURSE IT...IT...

I-I-I HAD A F-FEELING HE WASN'T AN ORDINARY K-K-KID...!

WHATCHA TALKIN' ABOUT?

HUH? WHAT?

138

Y-YOU'RE RIGHT... *BUT...*

W-WELL... YEAH...

C'MON! WHAT?!

SHOW HIM THE FULL M-MOON... THEN WE'LL KNOW...

WE G-GOTTA TEST IT...

JUST DON'T LOOK THERE, OKAY, GOKU!? JUST DON'T LOOK *THERE,* OKAY?!

TH-THAT WAS TOO CLOSE! WE CAN'T LET HIM LOOK...!

IF BY SOME TINY CH-CHANCE IT'S *TR-TRUE...* TH-TH-TH-THEN...

WAK!! Y-YOU'RE RIGHT!!

WHERE ?

WHOOPS...

I DID IT AGAIN.

Y-Y-Y-YOU'RE *OK*? N-NOTHING'S WRONG...?

WRONG HOW?

141

NEXT: The All-New Goku!!

152

156

158

OF COURSE !!!

L-LORD YAMCHA-- HIS *TAIL*-- HIS WEAKNESS !!

OH !!

B-BUT DOES HE HAVE THE SAME WEAKNESS IN *MONSTER* FORM?! OH, WELL--!!

NGH

VYOO

EH?!
EH?!

BOM!

AYE-
AYE
!!

QUICKLY,
PU'AR!!
TURN
INTO A
PAIR OF
SCISSORS
!!

ONE THREAT CUT OFF...BUT THAT'S HARDLY THE LAST OF OUR *TALE*!! (GET IT? *TALE...TAIL*?!) WHAT'S NEXT?!

NEXT TIME: *Adventure's End!?*

OKAY...REICH PILAF, PRISON, FULL MOON, MONKEY MONSTER, RAMPAGE, ESCAPE, SCISSORS, TAIL...THAT GETS US THROUGH ONE NIGHT! NOW LET'S RUSH AHEAD TO THE NEXT MORNING...

Tale 23
Separate Ways

SHEESH... WHAT THIS DOPE PUT US THROUGH...

YAWW...

PHEW... FINALLY... SUN-LIGHT...

SO WHAT *IS* HE...SOME KINDA SPACE ALIEN?

GUESS WE SHOULDN'T TELL HIM *HE* WAS THE MONSTER THAT SQUASHED HIS GRANDPA...

HE GOT US OUT OF PRISON, DIDN'T HE?

OH, CUT HIM SOME SLACK.

HEY! HE'S WAKING UP!

THANK GOODNESS...

WHATEVER HE IS...WITHOUT THAT *TAIL* HE'LL NEVER BE DANGEROUS THAT WAY AGAIN.

YO. 'MORNING.

MMBLE MMBLE...

HYAAW...

164

165

166

TEE HEE! WHO NEEDS DRAGON BALLS ANY MORE?

...LET'S HUNT DRAGON BALLS AGAIN, 'KAY?!

HUH?

AN' NEXT YEAR...

✳ GAG CHOKE BLEH *PTUI* GLAK ✳

?

NOT *MEE-EEE* ♡

ONE YEAR FROM NOW, PRESS THIS-- AND YOU SHOULD GET A SIGNAL!

NO PROB... I'LL GIVE YOU THE DRAGON RADAR!

THANKS!

I DON'T KNOW HOW TO TRACE IT!

SO HOW'M I GONNA FIND THE BALL GRAMPA LEFT ME?

HO!

SHALL WE GO-- SWEETEST ?!

IN THE MEANTIME, WE'LL ALL COME VISIT YOU!

GOKU, I HOPE YOU BECOME AS GREAT AS THE INVINCIBLE MASTER HIMSELF!!

ME TOO !!

172

Next: *The Price of Power*

Tale 24 • The High Price of Education

AFTER PARTING WITH BULMA AND CO.,
SON GOKU RACES ON CLOUDBACK TO THE
HERMITAGE OF KAME-SEN'NIN, WHERE HE HOPES
TO RECEIVE ADDITIONAL TRAINING...

HYUUUUU―N

I'VE NEVER SEEN IT FROM *ABOVE* BEFORE!

HEY, I'M CLOSE TO MY HOUSE!

MAN, I'M STARVING--!!

GUESS IF I'M GONNA BE STAYIN' WITH THE TURTLE GUY I SHOULD BRING MY FUTON AND STUFF.

HYUUUN

DON'T SCARE ME LIKE THAT!

EESH... IT'S ONLY YOU...

WONNG WONNG

...

HEH HEH HEH

Come on! A-one-an'-a-two--

JUST GIVE ME A MINUTE...

WHOA, WHOA!!

I CAME TO GET TRAINED.

HUH. WHAT A WEIRD BOX TO KEEP FOOD IN.

PENGUIN 3

THE FRIDGE IS RIGHT OVER THERE. GO HELP YOURSELF.

BUT I'M HUNGRY.

184

WHOA, WHOA, WHOA!!

COOL! THAT'S *EASY!!*

ONE O' THOSE ONES WITH NO WEE-WEE'S WHO'S ALWAYS WORRYIN' ABOUT HOW THEY LOOK...RIGHT?

WELL... YES...

JUST TO MAKE ABSOLUTELY SURE... DO YOU *REALLY* KNOW WHAT A "HOTTY" IS?

I THINK WE'D BETTER START AT THE BEGINNING...

THIS IS GETTIN' COMPLICATED... WHAT'S "BUSTY IS BEST" MEAN?

SHE'S GOT TO HAVE SPUNK AND CHARM... AND, OF COURSE, BUSTY IS ALWAYS BEST.

BUT EVEN THOSE WONDERFUL FEATURES AREN'T *EVERYTHING*, YOU KNOW...

186

187

W-WELCOME!!

OKAY, OLD TIMER, I GOT ONE--!!

...

WHADDYA WANT WITH ME?

UH... H-HELLO...

SHE'S FULL O' SPUNK, HUH?!

NEXT: *Cue Ball, Corner Pocket*

COMPLETE OUR SURVEY AND
LET US KNOW WHAT YOU THINK!

☐ Please do NOT send me information about Gollancz Manga, or other Orion title, products, news and events, special offers or other information

Name: _____

Address: _____

Town: _____ County: _____ Postcode: _____

☐ Male ☐ Female   Date of Birth (dd/mm/yyyy): ___/___/_____
                     (under 13? Parental consent required)

What race/ethnicity do you consider yourself? (please check one)

☐ Asian   ☐ Black   ☐ Hispanic

☐ White/Caucasian   ☐ Other: _____

Which Gollancz Manga title did you purchase?
☐ Case Closed Vol 1   ☐ Case Closed Vol 2   ☐ Dragon Ball Vol 1
☐ Dragon Ball Vol 2   ☐ Fushigi Yûgi Vol 1 ☐ Fushigi Yûgi Vol 2
☐ Yu-Gi-Oh! Vol 1   ☐ Yu-Gi-Oh! Vol 2

What other Gollancz Manga do you own?
☐ Case Closed Vol 1   ☐ Case Closed Vol 2   ☐ Dragon Ball Vol 1
☐ Dragon Ball Vol 2   ☐ Fushigi Yûgi Vol 1 ☐ Fushigi Yûgi Vol 2
☐ Yu-Gi-Oh! Vol 1   ☐ Yu-Gi-Oh! Vol 2

How many anime and/or manga titles have you purchased in the last year?
How many were Gollancz Manga titles?

Anime	Manga	GM
☐ None	☐ None	☐ None
☐ 1-4	☐ 1-4	☐ 1-4
☐ 5-10	☐ 5-10	☐ 5-10
☐ 11+	☐ 11+	☐ 11+

Reason for purchase: (check all that apply)
- ❏ Special Offer
- ❏ Favourite title
- ❏ Gift
- ❏ In store promotion If so please indicate which store: _____
- ❏ Recommendation
- ❏ Other _____

Where did you make your purchase?
- ❏ Bookshop
- ❏ Comic Shop
- ❏ Music Store
- ❏ Newsagent
- ❏ Video Game Store
- ❏ Supermarket
- ❏ Other: _____
- ❏ Online: _____

What kind of manga would you like to read?
- ❏ Adventure
- ❏ Comic Strip
- ❏ Fantasy
- ❏ Fighting
- ❏ Horror
- ❏ Mystery
- ❏ Romance
- ❏ Science Fiction
- ❏ Sports
- ❏ Other: _____

Which do you prefer?
- ❏ Sound effects in English
- ❏ Sound effects in Japanese with English captions
- ❏ Sound effects in Japanese only with a glossary at the back

Want to find out more about Manga?
Look us up at www.orionbooks.co.uk, or www.viz.com

THANK YOU!
Please send the completed form to:

Manga Survey
Orion Books
Orion House
5 Upper St Martin's Lane
London, WC2H 9EA